THE 12 WORST
TORNADOES OF ALL TIME

by Marcia Amidon Lusted

12 STORY LIBRARY

Photographs ©: Justin Hobson/CC3.0, cover, 1; *Lloyd's Steamboat Disasters*/PD, 4; Library of Congress, 5; ellepistock/Shutterstock.com, 6; Illustrated London News, 7; J.C. Strauss, 8; Strauss/US NOAA, 9; Jackson County Historical Society/CC, 10; Oklahoma City Air Logistics Center History Office/USAF, 11; Dmitry Chulov/Shutterstock.com, 12; University of Chicago News Office, 13; Bettmann/Getty Images, 14; Bettmann/Getty Images, 16; US NOAA, 17; Bettmann/Getty Images, 18; Tony Linck/Getty Images, 19; Happy Owl/Shutterstock.com, 20; Pavel Rahman/Associated Press, 21; Jeff Roberson/Associated Press, 22; FEMA, 23; Cammie Czuchnicki/Shutterstock.com, 24; diane39/iStockphoto, 25; Pavel Rahman/Associated Press, 26; Sergei25/Shutterstock.com, 27; Justin Hobson/CC3.0, 28; Cammie Czuchnicki/Shutterstock.com, 29

Library of Congress Cataloging-in-Publication Data
Names: Lusted, Marcia Amidon, author.
Title: The 12 worst tornadoes of all time / by Marcia Lusted.
Other titles: Twelve worst tornadoes of all time
Description: Mankato, MN : 12-Story Library, [2019] | Series: All-time worst
    disasters | Includes index. |
Identifiers: LCCN 2018011834 (print) | LCCN 2018025643 (ebook) | ISBN
    9781632356604 (ebook) | ISBN 9781632355416 (hardcover : alk. paper) | ISBN
    9781632356062 (pbk. : alk. paper)
Subjects: LCSH: Tornadoes--Juvenile literature. | Severe storms--Juvenile
    literature.
Classification: LCC QC955.2 (ebook) | LCC QC955.2 .L87 2019 (print) | DDC
    363.34/923--dc23
LC record available at https://lccn.loc.gov/2018011834

Printed in the United States of America
Mankato, MN
June 2018

About the Cover

An EF5 tornado approaches the town of Elie in the Canadian province of Manitoba on Friday, June 22, 2007.

Access free, up-to-date content on this topic plus a full digital version of this book. Scan the QR code on page 31 or use your school's login at 12StoryLibrary.com.

Table of Contents

Tornado Twists Its Way through Mississippi City

It was after noon on May 7, 1840, in Natchez, Mississippi. A thunderstorm had just passed through the city. People sat on their porches enjoying a cooling rain. No one could know a tornado was coming

Their first warning was a huge roar. It came from the nearby Mississippi River. The approaching tornado churned the water into giant waves.

Steamboats were scattered and smashed. People on board were thrown into the air. Most drowned upon falling into the water. Some boats sank to the river bottom.

The tornado's path was one mile (1.6 km) wide. The twister carried debris as it traveled. Uprooted trees and fragments of boats swirled through the air. In the city, houses

Only four men survived when the steamboat *Hinds* was sunk by the tornado.

TORNADO AT NATCHEZ.

LIBERTY ADVOCATE.

MES M. SMILEY, Editor.

LIBERTY, (ML.) THURSDAY, JUNE 18, 1840.

VOL. 5.—NO. 25.

The *Liberty Advocate* reported the details of the tornado on June 18, 1840.

TORNADO AT NATCHEZ.

[From the Vicksburg Sentinel.

BY MRS. V. E. HOWARD.

Lament—lament, for there hath been
An awful stroke of fate;
Lament—lament, for God hath made
A city desolate!

And none in that devoted place
Dreamed there was cause for fear;
They sat around their social boards,
Nor thought that death was near.

They heard a distant roaring sound,
The warning was in vain!
Till midnight darkness sudden fell,
And burst the hurricane!

were blown apart. Businesses were flattened. In just half an hour, the tornado left the city in ruins.

The official fatality count was 317 people. Most were merchants and passengers in boats. The actual number of dead was much higher. At this time in the American South, enslaved black people were not included in death counts. Newspapers estimated that hundreds died. So the Great Natchez Tornado probably killed more than 500 people. It is still the second-deadliest tornado in US history.

60
Number of flat-bottomed steamboats destroyed.

- No one had warning of the approaching tornado.
- The twister's path was one mile (1.6 km) wide.
- The official death count did not include enslaved people.

THINK ABOUT IT

Why do you think enslaved black people weren't included in the death toll? How does this reflect on the culture of the American South at this time?

2

Tornadic Waterspouts Devastate Italian Island

Tornadic and fair weather waterspouts form at the same time on the water.

165

Diameter in feet (50 m) of average waterspout.

- There are two types of waterspouts: fair weather and tornadic.
- In 1851, twin waterspouts transformed into destructive tornadoes.
- The twisters eventually moved out to sea.

THINK ABOUT IT

Why would a tornadic waterspout be more dangerous than a fair weather waterspout? What might it have to do with how each type is formed?

One of the worst tornadoes to hit Europe formed from two waterspouts. Waterspouts are also called sea tornadoes. They form when a column of air rotates above water. There are two types. Fair weather waterspouts develop on the surface of the water and grow upwards. Tornadic waterspouts descend from the sky during storms. They are more dangerous than fair weather waterspouts.

Two tornadic waterspouts hit the Italian island of Sicily in 1851. Waterspouts usually stay in the ocean. This pair went ashore and became powerful tornadoes. The twisters crossed the island. They tore apart homes and thrashed farmlands. Rain and hail added to the damage. An estimated 500 people were killed. Hundreds more were injured. After devastating Sicily, the twisters moved back to the sea.

Few eyewitness accounts exist of the Sicily tornadoes. A single tornado with two vortexes may have caused the damage. Two distinct funnels could also have been responsible. Whether one twister or two, the storm is among the deadliest in European history.

An artist's illustration of how the waterspouts looked once they hit land.

3

St. Louis, Missouri, Flattened by Powerful Twister

It was a quiet Wednesday afternoon in May 1896. St. Louis, Missouri, was warm and muggy. A thunderstorm was brewing. But the city had not had a severe weather disaster in 25 years. So no one expected what happened just after 5:00 p.m.

That's when a tornado struck. The twister

carved a three-mile (4.8-km) path through the city. Houses, factories, and churches were destroyed. Trees were pulled up by the roots and hurled. Iron fences were ripped up, twisted, and tangled. The winds even drove a shovel six inches into a tree trunk.

One structure that was supposed to be tornado-proof could not withstand the storm. The Eads Bridge was

The Eads Bridge was severely damaged.

At least 17 people were killed at this corner, including a woman who ran to warn them to flee.

constructed of stone and steel. That did not stop winds from tossing many of its stone blocks 100 feet (30 m).

The twister killed an estimated 255 people. At least 1,000 more were injured. Many who survived lost their homes. Total damage across the city was estimated at $25 million, or almost $700 million in 2017 dollars.

CITY CENTERS

It is rare for a tornado to hit the center of a city. Cities generally take up a small area. Also, tornado-prone regions don't have as many big cities. St. Louis has been unlucky enough to have its city core damaged by tornadoes at least five times. It is the most tornado-afflicted city in the United States.

20
Number of minutes the tornado was on the ground.

- The tornado carved a three-mile (4.8-km) path through St. Louis.
- The Eads Bridge was partially destroyed.
- The tornado caused $25 million in damage, or almost $700 million in 2017 dollars.

4

Tri-State Tornado Batters Missouri, Illinois, and Indiana

The Tri-State Tornado struck on March 18, 1925. It destroyed parts of Missouri, Illinois, and Indiana. People in these states did not have warning. No technology existed to predict tornadoes. There was also no organized warning system. When people looked at a darkening sky, they couldn't know what would happen.

Half the population of Murphysboro, Illinois, was left homeless.

Just after 1:00 p.m., a tornado developed near Ellington, Missouri. It touched down briefly, but returned to the sky. People thought they were safe. Then the twister touched down again. This time, it stayed on the ground. The tornado traveled across the three states. It moved at a record-breaking speed of 62 miles per hour (100 km/hour). That was only its average ground speed. In some places, the twister

219

Length in miles (352 km) of the tornado's track.

- In 1925, there was no system to warn people of tornadoes.
- The twister was on the ground for three and a half hours.
- The disaster showed the need for better warning systems.

EARLY WARNING SYSTEM

In 1943, the National Weather Bureau developed the first early warning system for tornadoes. Local weather observers reported conditions that might lead to tornadic activity. Radar technology was also used. Forecasters could now identify and track threatening storms. With greater warning, more people escape harm during storms.

traveled as fast as 73 miles per hour (117 km/hour). It stayed on the ground for a record three and a half hours.

The Tri-State Tornado showed the need for better storm prediction technology. With no warning of the twister, people did not take shelter. Across the three states, 695 people died. More than 2,000 were injured.

Major Ernest Fawbush (left) and Captain Robert Miller made the first tornado forecast.

5

Twister Blasts Dhaka District of Bangladesh

Bangladesh is tornado-prone. Its geography and climate lead to frequent storms. Cold air from the Himalaya mountains meets hot and humid air from the Bay of Bengal. The resulting storms can produce devastating tornadoes. The twister that descended on April 17, 1973, was no exception.

The tornado struck the Dhaka district in central Bangladesh.

The Dhaka district is one of the most densely populated areas of the city.

Nearly all buildings were leveled in villages along the Kaliganga River. Uprooted trees crisscrossed the land. The official death count was 681 people. The unofficial count was more than 1,000. This weather event stands as the fourth-deadliest tornado in history.

The tornado in the Dhaka district formed from two funnel clouds. They merged into one larger twister. It traveled in a zigzag path

Tetsuya "Ted" Fujita, shown here with his Tornado Simulator, created the Fujita Scale.

of destruction. The twister was so powerful that it blew a docked boat 3,000 feet (914 m) from shore. It also picked up a 15-foot-tall (4.6 m) concrete structure and dropped it several feet away.

8
Number of villages that were almost completely destroyed.

- The geography and climate of Bangladesh result in frequent storms.
- The twister was formed from two funnel clouds.
- The tornado is the fourth deadliest in history.

MEASURING TORNADOES

Meteorologists use the Enhanced Fujita (EF) Scale to rate how severe a tornado is. The scale ranks tornadoes by wind speed and damage. An EF1 tornado has wind speeds from 86–110 miles per hour (138-177 km/hour). It can damage small sheds. An EF5 tornado has winds of 200 miles per hour or greater (322 km/hour). It can sweep houses away. Before 2007, scientists used something called the F Scale. F5 was the most severe. Today you might see a tornado rated F5 or EF5 or even F/EF5.

Enhanced Fujita Scale	
EF–0	65–85 mph winds
EF–1	86–110 mph
EF–2	111–135 mph
EF–3	136–165 mph
EF–4	166–200 mph
EF–5	>200 mph

6

Gainesville, Georgia, Leveled by Twin Twisters

One tornado can do extraordinary damage. But tornadoes often come in twos. A storm in Gainesville, Georgia, brought two twisters on April 6, 1936.

The first tornado hit the city at 8:15 a.m. A second twister developed just outside of Gainesville. The two funnels spun toward each other, meeting downtown. This new double tornado then moved through the city. A pants factory was destroyed. The heavy winds brought down its walls. A department store also collapsed. The timing of the storm added to the loss of life. Many people were working or shopping at the time. More than 200 were killed and 1,600 injured.

Help arrived quickly. First, 500 young cadets from a local military academy arrived. They kept order until the

Gainesville City Hall was completely destroyed.

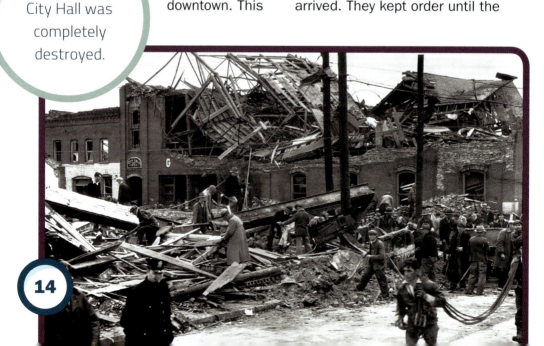

People begin to clear away the splintered wreckage after the disastrous tornado.

National Guard could come. Cleanup began immediately after the storm.

President Franklin D. Roosevelt cut short his Florida vacation to visit. He saw wooden buildings reduced to splinters. Businesses were burned down. Debris was everywhere. But the president also saw Gainesville residents working hard to rebuild. He was inspired by this resilience and gave a speech praising the town. Two years later, he returned to dedicate new city hall and courthouse buildings.

12

Number of tornadoes that touched down in the southern United States on April 6, 1936.

- The double tornado struck on a busy morning in Gainesville.
- Businesses across the city were destroyed.
- President Franklin D. Roosevelt was inspired by residents.

THINK ABOUT IT

Why do you think Gainesville residents were able to begin rebuilding their town so quickly? How would you react after losing a home or business?

15

7

Oklahoma Town Nearly Wiped Out by Tornado

The damage was described as being similar to an atomic bomb.

Woodward, Oklahoma, was almost completely destroyed by a massive tornado on April 9, 1947. The twister was one of at least six that descended on Texas, Oklahoma, and Kansas that day.

Woodward took the biggest hit. The tornado was nearly two miles (3.2 km) wide when it arrived at 8:42 p.m. It quickly destroyed the gas and electric plants. Residents were without power. Then more than 100 city blocks were leveled by high winds. The north and west sides of the city had the most damage. In all, more than 1,000 homes and businesses were destroyed. At least 95 people died.

$9.7 million

Amount of damage ($106 million in 2017 dollars) caused by tornadoes hitting Texas, Oklahoma, and Kansas on the same day.

- The tornado in Woodward was one of at least six twisters that descended on Texas, Oklahoma, and Kansas.
- More than 100 city blocks were leveled in Woodward.

Many Woodward residents found shelter before the twister arrived. Severe lightning and hail had caused them to seek safety. When all was calm, people left the shelters. Many found their houses gone. Buildings around the city continued to burn. Only a heavy downpour put them out.

During the night, temperatures fell below 40 degrees Fahrenheit (4°C). The rain turned to snow. Homeless residents suffered in the cold. The National Guard arrived, and people were given temporary homes in Army barracks.

Survivors search the remains of a two-story home.

8

New England's Worst Tornado Wreaks Destruction

June 9, 1953, was a beautiful summer day in Worcester, Massachusetts. People left work in the late afternoon. They went to watch ball games and have other summer fun. But dark clouds quickly moved in. It started to rain and hail. Weather forecasters worried a tornado might occur. But the technology for predicting one was new. Forecasters were afraid to panic

Neighbors comfort each other after assessing the damage of their homes.

people. So they chose not to issue a warning.

A twister was making its way through nearby towns. The funnel touched down in nearby Petersham. Then it snaked through the towns of Barre, Rutland, and Holden. When it hit Worcester at 5:09 p.m., the tornado was one mile (1.6 km) wide. Winds reached 335 miles per hour (539 km/hour). The tornado picked up cars. It blew down buildings. Trees were ripped out by their roots. Homes were blown into a nearby lake.

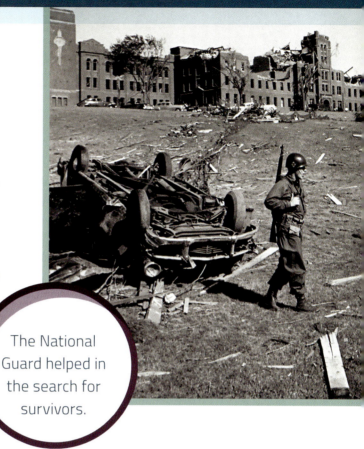

The National Guard helped in the search for survivors.

The twister was active in Worcester for 13 minutes. The total time it spent on the ground throughout the region was nearly 90 minutes. It caused $52 million in damage. That would be equal to $477 million in 2017 dollars.

At least 90 people died and an additional 1,300 were injured. It was the worst tornado in New England history. After that, forecasters changed how they did their work.

46
Length of the tornado's path in miles (74 km).

- Weather forecasters worried about a tornado but did not issue a warning.
- Winds up to 335 miles per hour (539 km/hour) were recorded.
- The twister spent nearly 90 minutes on the ground.

9

Twister Injures Tens of Thousands of Bangladeshis

Severe weather systems often produce multiple tornadoes. One system that hit Bangladesh injured tens of thousands of people. On May 13, 1996, multiple tornadoes struck the Jamalpur and Tangail districts. Winds of 125 miles per hour (201 km/hour) flattened 80 villages in less than a half an hour. Tree branches and pieces of corrugated metal roofing became deadly missiles. As debris flew, hailstones the size of softballs fell to the ground.

An estimated 700 people were killed in the storm. Many more Bangladeshis were injured. Approximately 32,000 sustained injuries. Local hospitals filled up quickly. People were refused medical help. Health officials said there was no room for them. Injured residents grew angry when they were not helped. Many blamed the Bangladesh government for not responding quickly enough after the tornadoes. There was reason for that.

The government did not send relief workers and medical supplies right away. Officials did not realize how many people were

Large hail injured thousands of Bangladeshis.

hurt and injured. Downed telephone wires in Jamalpur and Tangail made communication with the capital difficult. When officials understood the severity of the storm, they sent aid. More people began to get the help they needed.

30,000
Number of homes destroyed by the series of tornadoes.

- Multiple tornadoes caused damage in the Jamalpur and Tangail districts.
- An estimated 700 Bangladeshis died with an additional 32,000 people injured.
- The country's health system was not able to take care of all of the people who were hurt.

Injured villagers had to wait for care on hospital floors.

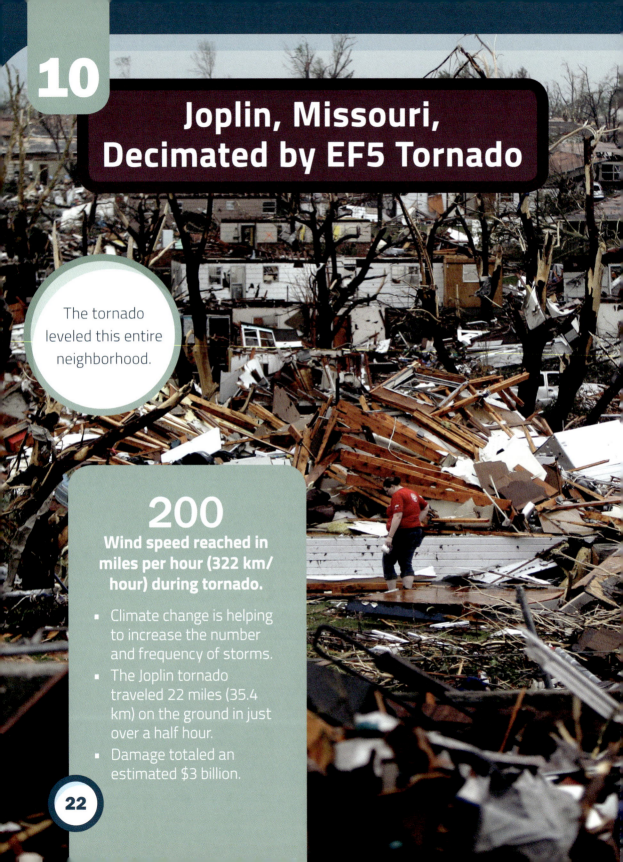

Joplin, Missouri, Decimated by EF5 Tornado

The tornado leveled this entire neighborhood.

200

Wind speed reached in miles per hour (322 km/hour) during tornado.

- Climate change is helping to increase the number and frequency of storms.
- The Joplin tornado traveled 22 miles (35.4 km) on the ground in just over a half hour.
- Damage totaled an estimated $3 billion.

Severe weather is on the rise throughout the world. Climate change is helping to increase the frequency and intensity of storms. Some of the worst tornadoes in the United States have occurred in the twenty-first century.

The force of the EF5 tornado imbedded a chair into a truck.

One that was especially destructive hit Joplin, Missouri, on May 22, 2011. The twister was on the ground for just over a half hour. Still, 157 people lost their lives. More than a thousand people were injured. The Joplin tornado is the deadliest in the United States since records have been kept.

The Joplin tornado traveled 22 miles (35.4 km). It swept homes off their foundations. Parking barriers weighing hundreds of pounds were tossed into the air. Cars were hurled into the air. Boards, tree limbs, and even a chair were embedded in walls. A bank was completely destroyed. Only its concrete vault was left standing. The storm cut a path one mile (1.6 km) wide. It went right through the center of Joplin. The tornado caused an estimated $3 billion in property damages.

A CLOSER LOOK AT THE DAMAGE

The Joplin tornado is notable for the damage it did to solid structures and objects. Buses and tractor-trailers were tossed, crushed, or rolled until they were unrecognizable. The steel trusses that supported building roofs rolled up like paper. Asphalt was torn from the surface of parking lots. And a rubber hose was driven through a tree.

Supercell Spawns Monster Oklahoma Twister

Supercell storms have deep rotating updrafts that can spawn tornadoes.

On the afternoon of May 20, 2013, a huge tornado struck the city of Moore, Oklahoma. It came at the end of three days of severe weather that produced other tornadoes in nearby counties and states. Storms brought large hailstones along with damaging winds.

$2 billion
Amount of property damage caused by tornado.

- The twister stayed on the ground for 39 minutes.
- The tornado was estimated to be one mile (1.6 km) wide.
- Forecasters' 16-minute warning allowed people to seek shelter.

The Moore tornado touched down at 3:00 p.m. and stayed on the ground for 39 minutes. The twister killed 24 people, including nine children. It injured 377 more. Its path was approximately one mile (1.6 km) wide and 17 miles (27 km) long. Winds reached 210 miles per hour (340 km/h). Such speed made it an EF5 tornado, the most severe category.

Oklahomans are used to severe storms. Moore's 2013 tornado was the seventh EF5 for Oklahoma. That is more than any other state. The city of Moore experienced another EF5 tornado 14 years earlier.

The National Weather Service gave Moore residents a 16-minute warning before the tornado struck. This allowed people plenty of time to find shelter. On average, forecasters can only give a ten-minute warning. That's because a warning can only be issued in certain situations. A spotter must see a tornado on the ground. Or Doppler radar must indicate tornadic rotation. The radar equipment tracking this storm was located very close to Moore. Forecasters were able to quickly see the developing tornado. Their speedy response likely saved lives.

Doppler radar can measure the location and velocity of a storm that may produce a tornado.

25

Bangladesh Hit by History's Deadliest Tornado

The world has seen many devastating tornadoes. So it takes a one-of-a-kind natural disaster to be named the deadliest twister in history. The tornado that struck the Manikganj district of Bangladesh on April 26, 1989, earned this title. At least 1,300 people lost their lives. Another 12,000 were injured.

It did not take long for this tornado to cause such devastation. Its path on the ground was only ten miles (16 km) long. Damage was restricted to a small area. But in that area, the destruction was complete. Buildings were demolished and trees uprooted. The towns of Saturia and Manikganj were left in rubble. Houses were easily flattened

There was total destruction in the town of Saturia.

A WARMING WORLD

Scientists have warned that devastating storms and severe weather will increase in the future. Warming global temperatures are heating up the earth's oceans and land masses. As a result, extra energy is being added to the atmosphere. This energy can help to increase the number of storms. These weather events are also more likely to be intense.

because of their poor construction. Approximately 80,000 surviving Bangladeshis were left homeless. Many others lost businesses or crops.

Bangladesh has a shorter tornado season than many countries. It runs from mid-March to mid-May. Yet many of the deadliest storms occur here. The geography and climate of the country make storms common, including severe ones. Bangladesh does not have a quality early warning system or enough storm shelters. Also, many people live in heavily populated areas. Large numbers of residents are affected when storms hit.

2.3
Area in square miles (2.6 km) where all structures were destroyed.

- The devastating twister was on the ground for only 10 miles (16 km).
- Approximately 80,000 people were left homeless.
- The geography and climate of Bangladesh make storms common.

Staying Safe If There's a Tornado

- Identify the best place to go in your home if there's a tornado. Options could include a basement, an inside closet, or a bathroom with no windows. In a bathroom, take cover inside the bathtub.

- You can also crawl beneath a piece of heavy furniture, or remain in the center of a room on the lowest level of your home.

- Stay away from windows or sliding doors that might be blown inward by high winds.

- Use your arms to protect your head and neck from flying debris.

- If you live in a mobile home, leave immediately to find a sturdy shelter.

- Identify good sources of shelter outside your home before a tornado occurs. Community centers, schools, and other city buildings may be options in your area.

- If you are outdoors during a tornado, lie in a ditch or other low area and cover your head and neck.

- If you are in a car, get out immediately. Lie in a ditch and cover your head and neck. Do not take cover under a highway overpass.

Glossary

barracks
A set of buildings where soldiers live.

churn
When something, often a liquid, moves and stirs strongly.

corrugated
A surface shaped into parallel ridges and grooves, to make it stronger.

debris
Scattered pieces of wreckage.

fatality
A death caused by accident, war, or disease.

fragment
A small piece or portion of something.

funnel
Something that is shaped like a cone, wide at the top and narrow at the bottom.

meteorologist
A person who studies and forecasts the weather.

radar
A system that uses pulses of radio waves to find the location of ships, aircraft, and storms.

rubble
Broken remains or rough fragments of stone, brick, or concrete.

supercell
A thunderstorm with both strong updraft and downdraft winds. A supercell can cause hail, lightning, and often tornadoes.

vortex
A whirling mass of air or water, such as a whirlwind or a whirlpool.

For More Information

Books

Kostigen, Thomas M. Extreme Weather: *Surviving Tornadoes, Sandstorms, Hailstorms, Blizzards, Hurricanes, and More!* Washington, DC: National Geographic Kids, 2014.

Roker, Al. *Al Roker's Extreme Weather: Tornadoes, Typhoons, and Other Weather Phenomena*. New York, NY: Harpercollins, 2017.

Simon, Seymore. *Tornadoes: Revised Edition*. New York, NY: Harpercollins, 2017.

Tarsish, Lauren. *I Survived the Joplin Tornado, 2011*. New York, NY: Scholastic, 2015.

Visit 12StoryLibrary.com

Scan the code or use your school's login at **12StoryLibrary.com** for recent updates about this topic and a full digital version of this book. Enjoy free access to:

- Digital ebook
- Breaking news updates
- Live content feeds
- Videos, interactive maps, and graphics
- Additional web resources

Note to educators: Visit 12StoryLibrary.com/register to sign up for free premium website access. Enjoy live content plus a full digital version of every 12-Story Library book you own for every student at your school.

Index

About the Author

Marcia Amidon Lusted has authored more than 150 books and 600 magazine articles for young readers. She is also an editor and a musician. Marcia previously lived in the Midwest, where she often had to take shelter because of tornado warnings.

READ MORE FROM 12-STORY LIBRARY

Every 12-Story Library Book is available in many fomats. For more information, visit 12StoryLibrary.com